GW00368032

Amazing
CLEVER
CRAFTS

Lots of really crafty things to make!

HH
HERMES
HOUSE

First published in 2000 by Hermes House

Hermes House is an imprint of
Anness Publishing Limited
Hermes House
88-89 Blackfriars Road
London SE1 8HA

A CIP catalogue record for this book is available from
the British Library

The activities and projects in this book were created by:
Petra Boase – *Painting Fun*
Thomasina Smith – *Modelling Fun*
Sally Walton – *Making Things*

Publisher: Joanna Lorenz
Managing Editor, Children's Books: Gilly Cameron-Cooper
Senior Editor: Nicole Pearson
Editor: Louisa Somerville
Editorial Assistant: Jenni Rainford
Photography: John Freeman, Tim Ridley
Design: Caroline Grimshaw

Previously published as part of three larger compendiums: *The Really Big Book
of Amazing Things to Make and Do; The Outrageously Big Activity, Play and
Project Book; The Ultimate Show-Me-How Activity Book*

10 9 8 7 6 5 4 3 2 1

Foreword

If you feel like being creative, then look no further! In here you'll find loads of craft ideas using all sorts of methods and materials, from salt dough to old tin cans. Transform the way you look with a veg-printed T-shirt and peanut-and-pasta jewellery. Give your room a make-over with a pretty butterfly mobile, a funky painted plant pot and a wacky dog's-bone photo frame. And don't forget to treat your friends and family! There are lots of groovy gift ideas from animal ornaments and bubble-printed notebooks to a gigantic greetings card. Step-by-step instructions show you how to create all sorts of cool effects including stencilling and flick-painting, using little more than lots of colourful paints. You don't have to wait for a rainy day to get started – why not get crafty right now and see what happens!

Contents

Modelling Fun 72

Basic Techniques

Cutting Out a Circle

It is difficult to cut a circle out of thick card or cardboard. The best way to do it is to ask a grown-up to stab a small hole in the centre of the circle, using the point of a sharp pair of scissors. Make several small cuts outwards to the edge of the circle. You will now be able to cut around the edge of the circle quite easily.

Cut out towards the edge of the circle.

Then carefully cut around the circle itself.

Painting Straight Lines

Masking tape is very useful for this. Stick the tape along the line, then paint right up to it. You can paint a little over the edge. Wait for the paint to dry completely, then pull off the tape and you will have a perfectly straight line. This is a good way to paint shapes like triangles and diamonds.

Use masking tape to help paint straight lines.

Painting Plastic

To make paint stick to plastic surfaces, add the same amount of PVA glue as the amount of paint and stir well. If the mixture is too thick, add a little water.

Varnishing

PVA glue can also be used to make varnish, which will protect the surface of many of your projects. Mix the glue with one third the amount of water. The varnish will look a bit white when you paint it on, but when it dries it will be clear.

Mix PVA glue with water to make a varnish.

Painting Round Objects

It helps when painting an object, especially when it's curved, like an egg or a ball, to rest it in a holder. That way it won't roll around when it is drying. Plastic pots, mugs and egg boxes make excellent holders.

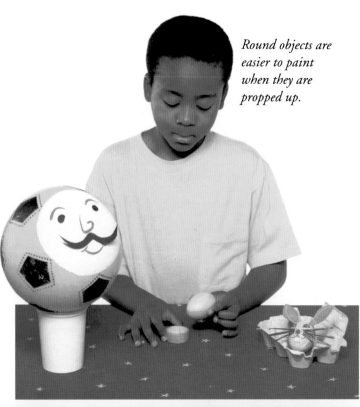

Round objects are easier to paint when they are propped up.

Tracing a Template

1 Place a piece of tracing paper over the template and secure it at the corners with tape. Carefully draw around the shape using a soft lead pencil.

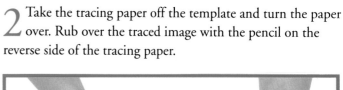

2 Take the tracing paper off the template and turn the paper over. Rub over the traced image with the pencil on the reverse side of the tracing paper.

3 Place the tracing paper on a piece of card, with the traced outline face up. Draw firmly over the outline to transfer the template on to the card.

4 Cut out your template. To use a template on paper, card or fabric, simply draw around the shape with a pencil, felt-tip pen or fabric marker pen.

You will need to use these templates for some of the projects in this book.

Safety First

• Be careful with sharp tools, glues and modelling materials. Keep them out of reach of young children.

• Point the tips of scissor blades away from you.

• Ask an adult to supervise when you are using an oven or stove. Wear oven gloves when handling hot items.

• Wait until baked items are cold before you touch them.

• Always ask permission to use an electrical appliance.

Star and Moon
Stencilled Gift Wrap

Template for the Stencilled
Cork Plate-mat

Flick-painted Starscape

Template for the mouth of the
Monster Sock Puppet

Spotty Dog-bone Picture Frame

Finger-painted
Flowers

Christmas Crackers

Finger-painted
Flowers

Making Things

Sally Walton

Introduction

Making things is great fun and very rewarding. It takes time and you have to concentrate to understand how things are put together. But all the hard work is worth it, because when you have made a rattlesnake or painted a flowerpot, it has some of your own very special magic in it. You will feel so proud, and everyone will admire your work. Once you understand how to make a mobile or cut flowers from felt, you will always know how it is done. Then you will be able to make up new designs of your own.

Look at the photographs of the children making up each project. They show you each stage and the words explain what they are doing. You can do it too, just follow what the children do.

Remember to ask a grown-up for permission before you begin making things. There are some projects that need a grown-up's help. Leave all the dangerous cutting-out to a grown-up, and never use a craft knife on your own as they are very dangerous. You may have to remind grown-ups that you are the one making things, because once they get started on the projects, they may not want to stop!

Be a crafty collector

We all like to recycle as much as possible. Once you start making things, you will be watching out to see what can be saved from the dustbin and made into a toy or a gift. You will need a good strong box for your collection and some-where to store it. If you save milk cartons and yogurt pots, give them a good wash in soapy water and dry them well, otherwise they may get smelly. Old tins and bottles are often covered with labels which you will want to take off. The easiest way to do this is to fill a washing-up bowl with some warm water and soak the bottle in the water for approxi-mately ten minutes. The label should peel off very easily. Collect small cardboard boxes and tubes, lollipop sticks, safe-edged tins, straws, corks, string, shells, bottle tops and cotton reels.

It is important to know when to stop collecting. If you have enough recycled packaging to fill your box, then start making things!

Colourful materials

For some projects you may have to use materials which you don't have at home, such as coloured card, felt, tissue paper, beads, pipe cleaners and wrapping paper. If you buy something special for a project then always keep any left-over scraps as they are bound to come in handy for any other project in the future.

Keeping clean

When you make things you can also make a lot of mess! It is most important to start off by protecting your work surface with old newspapers. Or putting down a tablecloth that will wipe clean. Do this first, because once you get involved with a project, it is easy not to notice the mess that you are making.

Wear an overall, apron or a big, old shirt to protect your clothes when you are painting. Before you start, roll up your sleeves as high as possible as they have a habit of dangling in paint pots and glue!

Getting started

When you have decided which projects you are going to make, collect together all the materials and equipment you will need and lay them out on your work surface. You will then find it much easier to work.

Clearing up

When you have finished, always clear up and put away all your things. Ask a grown-up to help you if you need to, but don't just leave a mess behind. Keep your equipment in good order and you will be ready to make something else another day.

Giant Sunflower Card

Sunflowers are among the tallest plants that we grow in our gardens, and this card takes its unusual shape from them. A sunflower has bright yellow petals and a big, rounded brown centre packed with seeds. This is the special part of the card that Kirsty is making.

This card would make a lovely present for Mother's Day, or a special gift for your teacher. Envelopes this shape may be difficult to find, so wrap up your card as a present. That is, if you can bear to part with it!

Tricky and sticky

The seed centre is the trickiest part of the sunflower to make, but once you understand how it is done, you will be making them all the time. The most important thing to remember is that too much glue will spread through the fine tissue paper and stick the next layer as well, and then the pop-up won't work. So use a tiny dot of glue, carefully pinching the two pieces of tissue paper between your finger and thumb to stick them together.

If you want to have leaves with jagged edges ask an adult to cut them out with pinking shears.

YOU WILL NEED THESE MATERIALS AND TOOLS

Large piece of blue card plus yellow, brown and green tissue paper

Needle and thread

Also a ruler, pencil, scissors, table knife, PVA glue, matchstick and a glue spreader

1 Cut out the card to 22 x 56 cm (8½ x 22 in). Find the middle, and score the card using a blunt table knife against a ruler. Just press firmly, so that the knife dents the card.

2 Fold the brown tissue paper over so that you have 10 layers. Cut out a circle that measures about 10 cm (4 in) across. Use a needle and thread to sew a running stitch down the centre line.

3 Cut out the petals, leaves and stems. You will need a lot of petals, about 30 to start with, two stems and five leaves.

4 To make the centre, think of a clockface. Imagine that the stitches go from 9 to 3. Using the matchstick, put a dot of glue at 12 o'clock.

5 Fold over the first layer of tissue and pinch it together where the dot of glue is.

6 Then, make two dots on the next layer of tissue. These go at where the 10 and 2 would be on the clock. Pinch together to stick. The next dot goes on the 12 spot and after that the 10 and the 2 again. Keep going like this until you reach the last layer. Let it dry.

7 Draw a circle for the flower centre, and arrange the petals around it. Put a thin layer of glue on each one. Make two or three circles of petals.

8 Spread a stripe of glue down the centre line and stick the two stems on top of each other. Stick down the leaves and the flower centre in the circle.

Open up the card and there is your glorious sunflower.

Canal Boat

Canals are like roads made out of water. They were used to move all kinds of factory goods from one part of the country to another on long, low canal boats, called barges. A long time ago the canals were very busy, but now most factories use lorries or trains instead. People still use the canals and barges, but mostly as homes or for holidays. The barge people have always decorated their boats in the same way, using black, red, yellow and green paint. They would paint flowers and patterns on the barge itself and all their buckets, flower-pots, jugs and boxes. The skill of barge painting was passed down through families, and people took great pride in their painted boats.

YOU WILL NEED THESE MATERIALS AND TOOLS

 Tall milk or juice carton, with a pointed end

 Pegs

Cork

Bottle cap

Also scissors, ruler, pencil, black emulsion paint, white emulsion paint (optional), red acrylic paint, paintbrushes, PVA glue, strips of white paper 1 – 1.5 cm (about ½ in) wide, felt-tipped pens and acrylic varnish (optional)

Beautiful barges

Edward has decorated this barge in the traditional colours, but using felt-tipped pens to make the patterns. Every barge has a name, usually a pretty girl's name, like Jenny-Wren or Lindy-Lou. Choose a name for your canal boat.

1 Cut the carton in half lengthways. One half will be the boat. Cut off the ends of the other half, to leave a rectangle of card. This will be the roof of the barge.

2 To make the roof, measure 1.5 cm (about ½ in) either side of both the existing creases and score lines with a blunt pencil and ruler. The lines will make it easier to fold the card.

3 Paint the outside of the boat black and the inside too if you wish. The top can be painted white first. This will make the red much brighter. If not, just give the top two coats of red acrylic paint.

4 Fold the roof along the lines and glue the edges to the inner sides of the boat. Peg until the glue is dry.

5 Ask a grown-up to cut a cork in half lengthways. Paint the two halves black. When they are dry, glue one half across the back of the boat and one onto the back of the roof. Glue the bottle cap onto the front of the roof, as a funnel.

6 Decorate the paper strips with felt-tipped pens. Use red, yellow and green to make patterns, and write the name of your barge on the long strips if you wish. Draw windows and some flowers for the top, as bright and bold as you like.

7 Stick all the paper strip decorations to the boat with PVA glue. If you want to put the boat in water, give it a coat of acrylic varnish for protection.

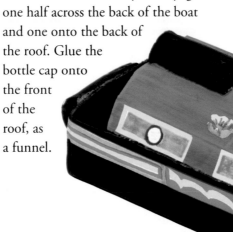

A real work of recycled art.

Stencilled Cork Place-mat

Make this place-mat, and brighten up the dinner table, even before the food arrives. It looks so good that the whole family will want one, and you will have to make a matching set. Start by making one for yourself. Ephram has used a carrot design for his mat. He could make a set using different vegetable stencils for each mat.

Stencilling technique

Stencilling is great fun and easy to do if you remember two simple rules. Always hold the stencil firmly in place with your spare hand and never use too much paint on your brush. The paint needs to be thick, so don't mix any water with it. Dip your brush in and then dab it on a piece of kitchen paper before you stencil on the cork tile. Use a different brush for each colour.

The felt backing will protect the table surface and also strengthen the thin cork and stop it breaking if you bend it. If you like a glossy surface, finish off your mat with a coat of acrylic gloss varnish, or PVA glue and water mixed three parts to one. This will add a tough, wipe-clean surface to the mat.

YOU WILL NEED THESE MATERIALS AND TOOLS

Unsealed cork floor tile and orange felt

Pencil, tracing paper, card from a cereal box, to make your stencil and template

Also a ruler, craft knife, scissors, black marker pen (not water-colour), thick, soft stencil brush, acrylic paint – orange and green, kitchen paper towel, acrylic varnish, PVA glue and a paintbrush

1 Using a pencil and ruler, measure and draw a line about 10 cm (4 in) in from the cork tile edge. Ask a grown-up to cut this strip off for you with a craft knife.

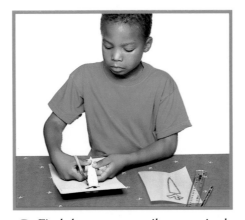

2 Find the carrot stencil pattern in the introduction, trace it onto the card and cut it out. Use the scissors to make a hole in the middle of the design, and then cut towards the outside edge. Move the card towards the scissors as you cut.

3 Make a template of the zig-zag border from the card. It should be the same length as the long side of the mat. Use the black marker pen to draw around it and colour the shape in. Fill in the corners to make triangles.

4 Stencil the carrots, starting with the one in the middle. Work from the stencil card inwards towards the centre, using a light dabbing movement. Always dab the paint from the pot onto a kitchen paper towel before using the brush on the cork. Use the paint very sparingly. You can always go over it again to add more colour, but too much at first will make blobs. Wipe the back of your stencil before painting the next carrot. The paint will dry quickly, but wait until it has done so or you may smudge the pattern.

5 To protect the design, either coat it with a glossy acrylic varnish or a coat of PVA glue mixed with water, three parts to one.

7 Spread the felt with PVA. Make sure that you reach right up to the edges. Stick this to the back of the cork.

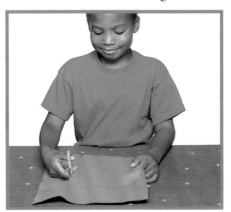

6 Cut the orange felt so that it is the same size as the mat.

More Stencilling Ideas

If you are more likely to eat your dinner from a tray, then you could paint it in the same way. If you have an old tray at home, ask whether you may decorate it. A wooden tray will need rubbing down with sandpaper first, and a tin tray may need a coat of gloss paint before you stencil it. You could use fabric paints to stencil onto plain dinner napkins, or just stencil paper ones with acrylic paint.

Butterfly Mobile

The butterflies in this mobile are made from mussel shells. You may not live near a beach where mussel shells can be collected, or have a garden where butterflies flutter about, but you can make this mobile that has a little bit of seaside and countryside in it.

If you have never tasted mussels before, this may be a chance to try them. Most fish-mongers sell mussels in their shells. When the mussels have been eaten, the shells are left, stuck together in the middle and already looking like butterflies. Scrub them well in warm soapy water.

YOU WILL NEED THESE MATERIALS AND TOOLS

7 mussel shells

Squeeze-on fabric paints, glitter, pearl or slick types

Gold paint and paintbrush

Pipe cleaners

Also 2 wooden boards, tin of paint for a weight, scissors, all-purpose clear adhesive, thin length of dowelling or garden cane, painted gold, and nylon thread

Fluttering in the breeze

Mobiles can be very relaxing to watch. Hang yours up above your bed and you will be able to drift off to sleep watching the butterflies gently turning in the air. Follow what Tania and Jade are doing and you will have a lovely mobile of fluttering butterflies.

1 Don't try to open out dry mussel shells, or they will come apart. Instead, soak the shells in warm water overnight. Open them out gently and place them face down on a board. Cover with another board and weigh it down with something heavy, such as a tin of paint.

2 When the open shells have dried, decorate each one with a different pattern using the squeeze-on fabric paints. Practise on paper first to get the feel of squeezing the paint from the tubes. Look at pictures of butterflies – you will see how many different patterns you can use on your shell butterflies.

3 When the fabric paint is dry, turn the shells over and paint the dark side with gold paint.

4 Cut up a pipe cleaner to make butterfly bodies about 4 cm (1½ in) long. Use glue to stick them in place.

5 Put a drop of glue 1 cm (½ in) in from each end of the stick, then knot the nylon thread over one of the dots. The glue stops the thread from slipping, making the knot easier to tie. Measure roughly double the length of the stick and cut and knot the nylon onto the glue dot at the other end. This is what the mobile hangs from.

6 Put seven dots of glue along the stick, 6 cm (2½ in) apart, and tie lengths of nylon over each dot. Tie the other ends of the nylon around the pipe-cleaner heads of each butterfly. Arrange them at different heights. It is very easy to tangle up the nylon threads so take care to keep each butterfly and its thread separate.

7 Seven very rare butterflies.

Butterflies Everywhere

It would be most unusual to buy just seven mussels from the fishmonger, so

you will probably have some left over. Decorate the shells with the paints and leave them to dry. Fix the bodies on as you did before and then glue them onto the corners of a picture frame or a mirror.

21

Feather Head-dress

The great Indian chiefs of North America wore head-dresses made from eagle feathers. They painted the feathers with patterns and each one had a special meaning, telling people how brave they were and how many battles they had won. Some chiefs wore head-dresses that reached all the way down their backs, from head to feet, called trailer war bonnets. When they held important gatherings or fought wars between the tribes, they would wear their feathers to show how brave and fierce they were. All the tribes understood the meaning of the feathers.

YOU WILL NEED THESE MATERIALS AND TOOLS

Piece of corrugated cardboard

Beads

String

Pasta quills

Pegs

Feathers, large and small

Elastic

Also scissors, ruler, white paper, PVA glue and felt-tipped pens

Magic feathers

Thomas and Edward are making this feather head-dress from seagull feathers, pasta quills, corrugated cardboard, beads and string. You can use any large feathers, so keep a look out when you go for a walk in the park or by the sea. If you live near a farm you can collect chicken or duck feathers.

Medicine men wore their feather head-dresses when they used their special powers, so perhaps you could wear yours and do a rain dance or, even better, a sunshine dance!

1 Cut the corrugated cardboard into a strip 4 cm x 25 cm (1½ x 10 in) and two discs 6 cm (2½ in) across. Cut white paper to match.

2 Glue the paper to the cardboard strip. Draw the beadwork pattern onto it with felt-tipped pens.

3 Glue the two paper discs to the cardboard discs. Decorate them with beadwork patterns.

4 Cut two lengths of string 18 cm (7 in) long. Thread beads onto each end of the string and make a knot below them.

5 Dip the end of a small feather in the glue and use it to push the middle of the string up into a channel in the corrugated card disc. This is quite fiddly so ask a grown-up for help if you find it difficult.

6 Place a pasta quill on each large feather and push the ends down into the channels in the decorated cardboard strip. Arrange the biggest ones in the centre, using smaller ones towards each side.

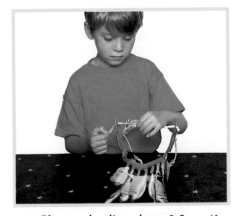

7 Glue on the discs about 2.5 cm (1 in) from each end. Peg the pieces together until the glue has dried. Make a hole at each end of the strip and thread elastic through to fasten at the back.

Beautiful Beadwork

The North American Indians made wonderful clothes and jewellery from beads, feathers and strips of leather. They believed that every living thing on Earth was precious and many of the patterns they used for beadwork or weaving told stories of nature and the lives of their ancestors. Ask at your library for a book about them, and copy the beadwork patterns to make pictures using felt-tipped pens or crayons. Try making jewellery from strips of chamois leather (we use it for car washing) threaded with beads and tubes of pasta, like macaroni. And don't forget to do that sunshine dance!

Jewellery Box

Some packaging is just too good to throw away. If you have a baby sister or brother, there may be some empty "wet wipes" boxes which have hinged lids and a clasp to keep them shut. You can decorate them with pieces of felt and make a very special box to keep your jewellery in. Felt is easy to cut, and craft shops sell squares 30 x 30 cm (12 x 12 in) as well as small bags of scraps in different colours.

The zig-zag edge is made by using special scissors called pinking shears. Dressmakers use them, so ask a grown-up who you know does a lot of sewing if they have a pair you can borrow. Felt is such fun to cut out any-way, so if you don't have pinking shears just cut your own fancy edges with scissors.

This box belongs to ...
Everyone has favourite colours, so choose the ones you like best when you cover the box. Fabric paints come in all colours and are either pearly, puffy or shiny when they dry. You will need to practise writing to avoid making blobs. Kirsty is making a box for her friend Maria. You could write your name instead. Try it out a few times on differ-ent pieces of felt, and choose your best effort to stick on the box.

1 Make paper templates by drawing around the top, long and short sides of the box. Cut them out, but make the patterns a bit smaller if your box has raised edges like this one.

2 Use pins to hold the patterns and felt pieces together. Choose different colours of felt for the top and sides of the box.

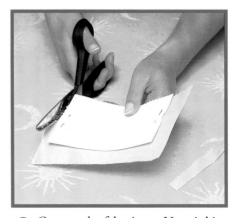

3 Cut out the felt pieces. Use pinking shears if you have them, or ordinary scissors if not. If you use pinking shears ask a grown-up to cut out the pieces of felt for you.

4 Stick the felt to the top and all the sides of the box.

5 Cut out circles of felt, about 4 cm (1½ in) across for the flowers, and smaller ones for the flower centres. Stick the centres down and snip towards the centre to make petals. Cut out some flower stems too.

6 Glue the flowers to the top and sides of the box.

7 Using a paintbrush, write your name on a piece of felt with fabric paint. Try writing in small dots if lines seem too difficult.

Now that you have made it, you will probably need some new pieces of jewellery to go in your jewellery box!

Fun with Felt

If you enjoy snipping and gluing felt you could make a cover for your diary or a folder. Measure the shape and cut the background coloured felt to fit. Cut out shapes and patterns, letters and numbers, and glue them onto the background. Always make sure that the glue is spread evenly across the felt and right up to the edges.

Felt can be used on its own to make things too. A bookmark is useful. Just cut a long strip and snip 1 cm (½ in) into the ends to make a fringe.

Painted Flower-pot and Saucer

Everyone loves a gift that has been specially made for them. You may not be ready to make a flowerpot yet, but you could certainly decorate one as a special present.

Indoor plants can look dull in plain clay pots, especially the leafy ones without any flowers. This bright red and yellow pattern that Roxy is painting is very easy to do and is just the thing to brighten up a winter windowsill.

Preparing your pots

Clay pots need to be sealed before you can paint them, and PVA glue can be brushed on to give a good waterproof paint surface. When you paint stripes around a shape like a flowerpot, it is hard to keep the lines straight. A good trick is to put a rubber band around the pot wherever you need a guideline. It makes a slightly raised line to paint up to and can be slipped off when the paint is dry.

YOU WILL NEED THESE
MATERIALS AND TOOLS

Houseplant

Clay flowerpot and saucer

Also PVA glue, to seal the surface of the pot, paintbrushes, acrylic paint – red and yellow, and a rubber band

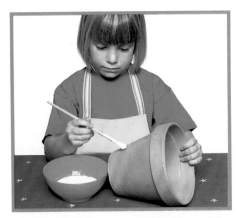

1 Mix up three parts PVA glue with one part water and brush this all over the flowerpot and the saucer. Leave them to dry.

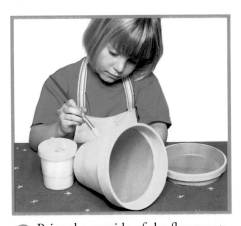

2 Paint the outside of the flowerpot and its inner rim and the outside of the saucer yellow. Mix acrylic paint with a little water, to make it thick and creamy. Leave it to dry and then paint on a second coat.

3 Stretch a rubber band around the flowerpot to mark the edge of the red section. Paint as shown in the picture. Leave the rubber band on until the paint is dry.

4 Make two red stripes with dots in-between them around the outer rim of the pot.

5 Paint the rim of the saucer red. Allow to dry. Then decorate the saucer with red spots on the yellow background and yellow spots on the red background.

6 Make yellow dots along the red stripes at the top of the pot. Paint yellow stripes down to the bottom edge, over the red. Paint big red dots in the middle and, when dry, put in smaller yellow dots. When all the paint has dried, seal the pot with the same PVA glue and water mixture that you started with in the first step.

A little bit of sunshine to put on the windowsill.

Go Potty Painting Pots!

Flowerpots come in all sizes and there are many different ways to paint them. Spots, stripes, wavy lines, diamonds, flowers – these are a few of the different shapes that you could use to make patterns. Stars look great too. Try making a stencil out of a piece of card. Cut out the shape with scissors and hold it firmly against the pot. Paint through the stencil, being careful to use only a tiny amount of paint on your brush.

Cork Rattlesnake

This cork and bead snake has a slithery feeling and will curl up or wriggle along, just like the real thing. Rattlesnakes get their name from the rattle at the end of their tail. They curl up and shake the rattle, holding their heads ready to strike when danger approaches. The rattling sound warns all creatures to beware as the rattlesnake is very dangerous.

YOU WILL NEED THESE MATERIALS AND TOOLS

 10 winemaker's bored corks

 Coloured beads – large-holed

60 cm (24 in) of flat elastic 1–1.5 cm (about ½ in) wide

 Pipe cleaner
Rubber bands

Also paintbrushes, acrylic paints – green, black, red and yellow, ordinary cork, cut in half lengthways, PVA glue, scissors and acrylic varnish (optional)

Colourful crazy patterns

The corks used in this project have holes through the middle and are usually used for making home-made wines. You can buy them from large chemists and shops that specialize in winemaking equipment. Ordinary corks could be used, but you would have to ask an adult to drill holes through the middle of them for you.

Snake colours are brilliant and their patterns are exciting. Zig-zags, diamonds, stripes, swirls and spots are all very snaky. Look at what Reece and George have done and then have fun with your patterns and make a really unusual rattlesnake.

1 Paint all the corks green. Leave them to dry completely.

2 Paint the black pattern first. Then paint the red and yellow patterns in-between the black ones. Don't forget to decorate the ordinary cork that has been cut in half. This will be made into the mouth.

3 When the paint is dry thread the main body of the snake onto the elastic, with a bead between each cork. The corks are thicker at one end than the other. Make sure the tail cork tapers to the thin end.

4 Thread five or six beads onto the end of the snake to make the rattle. Tie a knot at the end.

5 Pull the elastic up through the snake. Don't pull it too tight though, because the snake must be able to wriggle and roll up. Thread two beads onto the pipe cleaner to make the snake's eyes. Cut off the extra pipe cleaner leaving 1 cm (½ in) to twist and secure the beads in place. Flatten out the elastic so it runs along the flat side of the cork and sticks out at the end. Place the pipe cleaner across the elastic.

6 Paste with PVA glue and put the other half of the cork on top. Hold the two pieces together with a rubber band until the glue is dry.

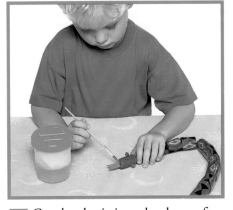

7 Cut the elastic into the shape of a forked tongue and paint red. The snake can be varnished with acrylic gloss or PVA glue diluted with water.

A slithery snake pet with no nasty nips.

Slithery Lizard

You could make a lizard out of corks. For the legs, ask a grown-up to make holes across two of the corks. Make the lizard up in the same way as the snake, then thread shorter pieces of elastic through the new holes. Thread three beads on each side and then a cork, with the wide end down. Add one more bead and tie a knot. Four corks added in this way will make four stubby lizard legs.

Peanut and Macaroni Jewellery

YOU WILL NEED THESE MATERIALS AND TOOLS

Peanuts in shells

Macaroni

Beads

Darning needle and shirring elastic

Also paintbrushes, acrylic paints – red, blue, black and yellow, a cup, acrylic gloss varnish (optional) and PVA glue

Who needs gold, silver and diamonds when you have macaroni and peanuts in the kitchen cupboard? You can make the bright and chunky necklace and bracelet very easily and all your friends will want to make them too.

The peanuts look great painted in very bright primary colours, and are light and comfortable to wear. The macaroni is perfect for threading and makes a good space between the peanuts. Use acrylic paints which dry in five minutes, and give the nuts a good glossy varnish to make them shine.

Miniature maracas

You will notice that when you wear the necklace you feel like dancing. That is because the nuts rattle in the shells as you move and it is like having lots of little maracas around your neck! You could make some ankle bracelets too and do a rattling, stamping dance. Ephram has made this necklace and bracelet for his friend Saadia.

30

1 Paint the peanuts different colours and leave to dry.

2 Mix some paint in a cup to colour the macaroni. Drop the macaroni in the cup and stir. Tip out and separate the pieces. Leave to dry.

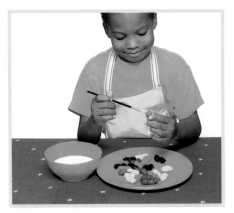

3 When they are dry, varnish the nuts and macaroni with acrylic gloss varnish or PVA glue and water mixed three parts to one. Leave to dry.

4 Use a darning needle to make holes through the middle of the peanuts. There is a hollow space between the two nuts, where the shell goes in at the "waist". Push the needle through both sides.

5 Measure around your neck and wrists and cut the shirring elastic just a bit longer. Thread the darning needle and tie a bead onto the end of the elastic.

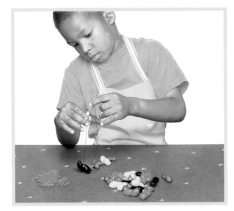

6 Thread one piece of macaroni, then one nut and repeat the colours in the same order until you reach the end of the elastic.

7 Finish with a piece of macaroni and then tie on a bead. Tie the two beaded ends together.

What Else Could You Thread?

Popcorn can also be threaded to make jewellery. You will need home-made popcorn that has no salt or sugar coating. You can paint and varnish it with acrylics, just as you did with the peanuts.

Thread the darning needle and push it through the middle of the popcorn, where the burst outer shell is, as this is the strongest part. When you have threaded enough for a necklace, cut the elastic and tie a knot. You could try combining the macaroni, monkey nuts and popcorn. There are also lots of pips and seeds that thread easily, so have a good look in the store cupboard. Ask a grown-up if it is all right and then get threading.

Doll's House

The next time you visit a supermarket, choose a good strong cardboard box from the check-out to use to pack the shopping. When the groceries are all put away, you can use the box to make this doll's house.

You will need a grown-up to help with the first stages. Never use a craft knife on your own as the blades are dangerously sharp. The step photographs show how the box is cut, and you can help with a ruler and pencil, measuring and drawing the cutting guidelines, just as Kirsty is doing here.

Paint the house and roof with a light-coloured emulsion paint, the sort that is used to paint walls at home. This will make a good base coat for felt-tipped pens.

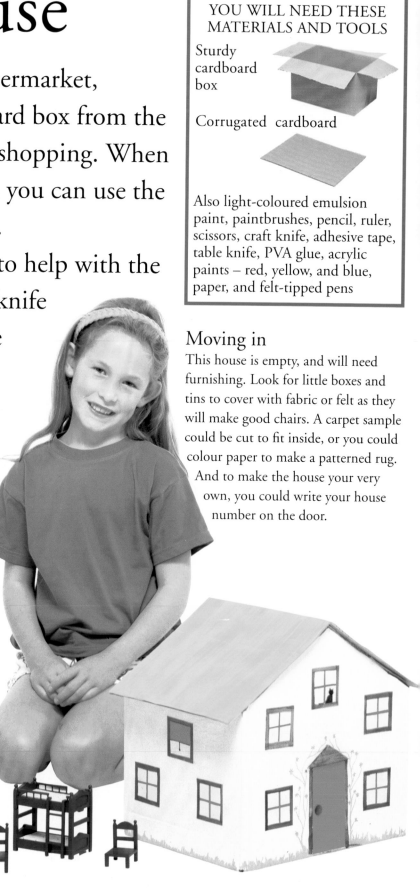

YOU WILL NEED THESE MATERIALS AND TOOLS

Sturdy cardboard box

Corrugated cardboard

Also light-coloured emulsion paint, paintbrushes, pencil, ruler, scissors, craft knife, adhesive tape, table knife, PVA glue, acrylic paints – red, yellow, and blue, paper, and felt-tipped pens

Moving in

This house is empty, and will need furnishing. Look for little boxes and tins to cover with fabric or felt as they will make good chairs. A carpet sample could be cut to fit inside, or you could colour paper to make a patterned rug. And to make the house your very own, you could write your house number on the door.

1 Paint the box. On both sides measure 10cm (4in) from the top. Find the middle point along the top edge. Join the dots and draw a triangle.

2 Ask a grown-up to cut out the shape of the house for you using big scissors or a craft knife.

3 The back of the house should be cut away so you can reach inside. Ask a grown-up to do this with the craft knife.

4 Use the side flaps to create the roof peak. Score the lines where they fold but don't cut right through. Stick the flaps down with adhesive tape.

5 To make the roof, measure the top of the box. Cut the corrugated cardboard so it is 2.5 cm (1 in) wider each side and 5 cm (2 in) longer at each end. Score down the central line with a table knife. Ask a grown-up to help you if you need to.

6 Bend the roof along the scored line. Paint the inside with PVA glue and place it on top of the house. When the glue is dry, paint the roof with yellow acrylic paint.

7 To make the windows, cut out squares of paper and paint the edges with blue acrylic paint. Cut out a front door and paint it red.

A pretty country house complete with cat, ready to be moved into and furnished.

Budding Architect

You could make lots of different buildings out of cardboard boxes. Perhaps you would like a garage to go with your house. You could even make a whole street of different buildings, including shops and a church.

Look for different sized boxes, such as shoe boxes, and other things. What could you use to make a post box, for example?

Pencil-pot Découpage

Pencils, pens and brushes roll off tables or slip down between the cushions of a sofa when you are concentrating hard on making pictures. You can organize yourself by making this pencil pot from a food tin with a ring-pull lid. Tin openers leave dangerously sharp edges, so be sure to choose the safer type with a ring-pull for this project.

The word découpage means "cutting out" in French. You cut out pictures and glue them to the object you are making. Furniture is some-times decorated in this way, and then given many coats of clear varnish. You can use clear acrylic varnish to give your pot a shine, or a mixture of PVA glue and water, mixed three parts to one.

YOU WILL NEED THESE MATERIALS AND TOOLS

Sheet of wrapping paper or other pictures

Empty tin, washed

Felt

Also blue paint, either acrylic or gloss, paintbrushes, scissors, PVA glue, soft cloth, acrylic gloss varnish (optional), small piece of corrugated cardboard and a pencil

Choosing your decorations

Jade has painted this tin blue and decorated it with cut-outs from a sheet of wrapping paper, but you could use the same method to make a pencil-pot to suit your own interests. Perhaps you have a comic-book character, pop star or sports person – someone whose picture you would like to see every day. Just cut out a combination of pictures that you like and glue them onto the painted tin. Take your time when cut-ting out, moving the paper to meet the scissors. It is a good idea to practise on a few spare sheets of paper before you cut out your most special pictures.

1 Paint the tin blue. Water-based paint is best, because you can wash your brushes under the tap. Acrylic will need two coats of undiluted paint.

2 Carefully cut out the motifs. The pattern looks best if you have two different sorts, such as butterflies and teddy bears.

3 Spread PVA glue over the back of each motif, making sure you reach all the outer edges. Otherwise the sides will curl up.

4 Stick down the motifs, using a soft cloth to flatten out any air bubbles. Arrange them around the tin with the same amount of space between them.

5 When the glue is dry, paint on acrylic varnish or a mixture of three parts PVA glue to one part water. The varnish can be gloss or matt.

6 Stand the tin on a piece of corrugated cardboard and draw around it. Cut out a circle, just inside the line, to fit into the base.

7 Draw a circle on the felt in the same way, but cut it out just outside the line. Stick the felt to the cardboard, then the cardboard to the pencilpot with PVA glue.

Your very own, very organized decorated découpage pencil-pot!

What Else Deserves Découpage

You can cut out and stick all sorts of motifs onto all kinds of surfaces, not just tins. Wooden boxes, trays and bedroom furniture can all be brightened up with paper cut-outs, but always ask permission from a grown-up first. If you find a black and white picture or pattern that would make a good border, you can photocopy it as many times as you need. Cut out and colour your photocopies, and then glue them on.

Birdwatchers

If you have ever seen birdwatchers, you'll have noticed that they are very quiet and slow-moving. Any sharp movements or noises would frighten the birds and they would fly away.

These binoculars are green so they are camouflaged as you creep around the park or garden birdwatching. Stay very still and the birds will come quite close. If you have a bird-bath or table in your garden, the birds that use it will be quite tame, so they might not mind even if they do see you watching.

Sunny all the time

These binoculars have a very special feature. They brighten up dull days, making the world outside look sunny, even when it's grey. George has found some sweets with yellow cellophane wrappers – just the thing to cover the ends of his binoculars.

YOU WILL NEED THESE MATERIALS AND TOOLS

Two toilet-roll tubes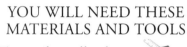

Green paper, ruler and pencil

Piece of yellow cellophane

Adhesive tape

Black plastic tape

Black cord

Also scissors, a wine cork, PVA glue, paintbrush, black acrylic paint and a rubber band

1 Cut out two squares of cellophane and tape them over one end of each cardboard tube. Ask a grown-up to help if you find this difficult.

2 Cut out two rectangles of green paper measuring 12 x 19 cm (4½ x 7½ in). Then cut a strip of paper to fit around the cork.

3 Ask a grown-up to trim the cork lengthways, so that one half has two flat sides. Paint the ends with black acrylic paint.

4 Take the strip of green paper and glue it around the cork. Paint on lines for the focusing winder.

5 Brush the pieces of green paper with glue. Line up with the tube ends without cellophane, then roll the tubes onto the paper.

6 Stick black plastic tape around the ends with the cellophane, then trim the paper and tape close to the cellophane ends.

7 Spread a stripe of glue along the side of one tube, and both flat sides of the cork. Assemble the binoculars, and hold them together with a rubber band until the glue is dry.

8 Push a hole through the sides of each tube, and thread the black cord through. Tie a knot on the inside.

Now you are ready to go birdwatching – and the weather looks just fine!

Monster Sock Puppet

Everyone has an odd sock somewhere around the house, waiting to be brought to life as a monster sock puppet. Try to find one that is brightly coloured and use a contrasting colour felt for the mouth and fins. Kirsty has practised her monster noises, because she is going to need them!

Pins and needles

If you have never used a sewing needle before, be sure to ask a grown-up to help you. Sewing is quite easy, once you know how, and you will not need to use a very sharp needle to sew through felt and sock material. A darning needle will do the job.

If you use pins to hold the mouth lining in place as you sew it, be very careful, because they are sharp. Always position them so their points are facing in the same direction around the monster's mouth. When you start to sew, work towards the heads, not the points, of the pins. Each time you reach a pin, remove it and put it back in a pin cushion or tin, so that nobody gets a sharp surprise!

YOU WILL NEED THESE MATERIALS AND TOOLS

Plain coloured sock

Felt, different colour from the sock

Darning wool and needle

Two large buttons

Also a pencil, tracing paper, paper, scissors, pins (optional), thread, PVA glue and a glue spreader

1 Trace the template for the mouth which you will find in the introduction. Cut it out to make a pattern. Put this on a folded piece of felt, so that the fold is along the straight edge of the pattern. Cut out the mouth and the other shapes. Just nip the felt to make zig-zags, spiky fins, and a tongue.

2 Turn the sock inside-out and cut along the toe seam and past it on both sides by about 5 cm (2 in). Measure the opening against the pattern for the mouth, to get the size right.

3 Pin the mouth lining into the toe end, flapping the top back, so that you can sew the lining in one flat piece. Sew along the seam using running stitches. Make a small cut along the fold of the mouth and poke the tongue through it, so that it sticks out on the other side. Sew the tongue in place.

4 Turn the sock right side out and sew on buttons for eyes. Use wool to do this, pushing the needle up from inside the sock, through the holes and back down again. Tie the ends of wool inside the sock.

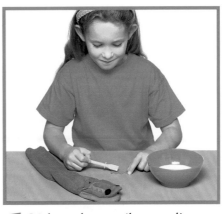

5 Stick on the nostrils, spreading PVA glue across the back of the felt, right up to the edges. Stick on the triangles and zig-zags in the same way.

6 Sew the long back fin along the centre of the monster's back, using black thread or wool. Be careful not to prick your hand with the needle.

Now is the time to use those monster noises that you have been practising!

Shark Alert!

There are all kinds of creatures to be made from odd socks. If you have a grey sock you could try making a shark. You will need grey felt for the fins and red for the mouth lining. Nice white teeth are a very important feature, so cut them from felt and fit them into the mouth at the same time as the lining. Think carefully as they will need to stick up from the shark's gums. So cut triangles and sew the flat ends into the mouth seam, leaving the pointy teeth to stick up in the mouth. To make the big back fin, cut two triangles and put a bit of cotton wool stuffing in-between them. Sew around the edges and then sew the base of the fin into the middle of the back.

Magnetic Fishing

This game is almost as much fun to make as it is to play. You could make it at your birthday party with each guest having a fish to decorate. The fish shape is very simple, but your decoration can be wild or realistic. Roxy and Rupert like bright colours for their fish. Have a look at some fish in a shop or borrow a book about fish from your library – there are so many beautiful patterns and colours to choose from.

Playing the game

There are many different ways of playing this game. Dangle your rod over the fish until you connect with one, then lift it up. To make it harder, try this blindfolded or write points on to the fish and add up each player's score at the end.

YOU WILL NEED THESE MATERIALS AND TOOLS

Fluorescent or coloured cardboard

Magnets   Paper clips

Also a pencil, tracing paper, card for the template, scissors, felt-tipped pens, string and bamboo poles

1 Draw a fish template on to card. Follow the instructions at the front of the book to trace and cut out your fish pattern.

2 Use the template to draw fish on the different coloured card. Hold the template firmly so that it does not move while you are drawing.

3 Cut out all of your fish, taking care to do this as neatly as possible, by following the lines of the template.

4 Decorate the fish with different coloured felt-tipped pens. Try out different patterns on them as well.

5 Attach the paper clips to the mouths of the fish. The magnets will attach themselves to these.

6 To make your fishing rods, tie a small magnet to a piece of long string.

7 Then tie each piece of string on to the end of one of the bamboo poles. Knot it tightly!

Other Magnetic Games

Magnetic fishing does not have to involve fish. You could make sets of different parts of the body – head; bodies, legs and arms. Some can be girls and some boys and their clothes can be as silly as you like. Put them all in a box with paper clips attached and take turns to fish for them. It will be like a game of picture consequences when you have to fit your person together. Alternatively you could fish for letters to make words, or pictures of food to make up dinners.

Roxy and Rupert have made a pond where they can go fishing.

Painting Fun

Petra Boase

Introduction

Painting is fun, but painting does not necessarily mean standing at an easel painting a picture of what you can see – although you can do that too if you want. The projects in this chapter show you how to have lots of fun with different sorts of paints on lots of different surfaces.

None of the projects in this section is difficult, although there are a few things you should do before you begin.

1 Carefully read through the list of materials you will need.

2 Read through the instructions and look at the photographs so that you have a clear idea of what you will be doing.

3 Assemble everything you need before you start on a project.

4 Some of the projects are messy and some aren't, but it is always a good idea to cover your work surface with newspaper, scrap paper or a piece of material. If you are working on a wipe-clean surface and doing one of the less messy projects, this is not essential, but it is a good idea to get into the habit.

5 Wear an old shirt or a painting overall and, when you have finished, always clear away everything you have used.

You may not want a grown-up around while you are being creative, but there are some things that you will need help with. Some of the projects call for sharp scissors and you may prefer a grown-up to do the cutting for you. Some types of card are easier to cut with a craft knife. These knives are very sharp and are quite tricky to use, so always get a grown-up to do any cutting with a craft knife. Always ask a grown-up to mix and thin oil paints for you as well. You can mix other kinds of paint such as water colour and poster paint yourself.

Wear an old shirt or painting overall

Before you begin, make sure you have everything you will need.

Colour mixing

You don't need a lot of different coloured paints to do the projects. It is easy to mix lots of colours as long as you have the three primary colours of red, blue and yellow.

Red + Blue = Purple
Red + Yellow = Orange
Blue + Yellow = Green

You can make different sorts of browns by mixing purple and orange, orange and green and purple and green.

If you start off with red, yellow and blue and, perhaps, white (with which you can make pink and pale shades of the other colours), you can easily add more colours as your pocket money allows. You will also need black paint for some of the projects so check before you begin.

Be careful when you use scissors.

44

Types of paint

Each type of paint is different and takes different times to dry. Always read the instructions on the pot or tube before you start.

Acrylic paint This is rubber-based, flat and opaque so that it covers large areas easily but does not have the shine of oil paint or the texture of water-based paint.

Fabric paint Fabric paint is necessary for painting or printing on textiles. Each type is different so read the instructions carefully and clean your brushes accordingly.

Oil paints These are very greasy and must be handled with care. Ask a grown-up to mix white spirit or turpentine with oil colours to thin them. Ask an adult to clean your brushes with white spirit or turpentine.

Poster paint This is water-based and is available either as a powder to be mixed with water, or ready-mixed.

Coloured inks These are available in a wide variety of colours. If you can't find any, or can't get a colour you want, you can use food colourings instead. Always make sure they are washable.

Poster paints

Fabric paints

Acrylic paints

Oil paints

Coloured inks

Star and Moon Stencilled Gift Wrap

If you have always wanted to make your own special gift wrap and matching greetings cards, now is your chance.

The moon and star shapes that Kirsty is stencilling are simple. She is only using gold paint, but you can use lots of different colours. If you want to stencil with lots of colours, use a different sponge for each colour and let each colour dry thoroughly before you add the next.

Stencilling technique

Stencilling is great fun and easy to do. For the best results, the paint needs to be thick, so don't mix any water with it. Do not use too much paint on the sponge, and apply it with a light dabbing movement. You can always go over it again to add more colour.

YOU WILL NEED THESE MATERIALS AND TOOLS

Tracing paper

Soft pencil

Thin card

Scissors

Coloured paper

Re-usable adhesive

Sponge

Gold paint

Palette or saucer

Ribbon

Hole punch

1 Using a soft pencil, trace the star and moon templates from the front of the book on to card.

2 Use the scissors to make a hole in the middle of the design, and then cut towards the shape. You should have three different stencils.

3 Place the stencils on the coloured paper. Secure them with re-usable adhesive. Dab the sponge in the gold paint and sponge over the stencils.

4 Let the paint dry, then move the stencils to another space on the paper and repeat. Continue until you have covered the whole sheet with gold moons and stars.

5 When the paint is completely dry, use the sheet of paper to wrap up a present. To make the gift extremely luxurious, add a gold ribbon and tie a bow.

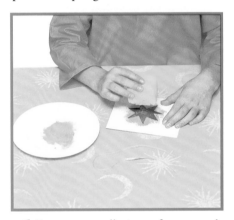

6 Cut out a small piece of paper and stencil it in the same way to make a gift tag for the present. Using a hole puncher, make a hole in the corner and slip a piece of gold ribbon through.

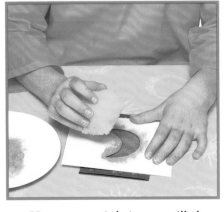

7 Here a moon is being stencilled on to a card for a different design.

A unique set of gift wrap for a very special present.

Christmas Crackers

Your family and friends will be delighted when you present them with these pretty crackers at the Christmas meal or at a party. You must plan this project in advance as you need a cardboard tube for each cracker.

Jessica is using traditional Christmas shapes and colours in her design, but you could choose your own instead.

Presents galore

If you are feeling generous you could also put a little gift inside each cracker, and perhaps write a joke to go inside as well. This should be done in step 7, when you have closed only one end of the cracker.

YOU WILL NEED THESE MATERIALS AND TOOLS

Tracing paper

Soft pencil

Coloured paper

Scissors

White paper

Re-usable adhesive

Palette or saucer

Sponge

Poster or acrylic paints

Toilet roll or other cardboard tube

Ribbon

PVA glue and a brush

1 Trace the holly leaf and Christmas tree templates from the front of the book on to coloured paper and cut them out.

2 Scatter the shapes over the white paper, sticking them down with a piece of re-usable adhesive. Your pattern can be regular or random.

3 Dab the sponge into one of the paints. Wipe off any excess on the side of the palette. Sponge over all the shapes on the paper.

4 Rinse the sponge out under the tap, squeezing it as dry as you can. Dab it in the second paint colour and sponge over the shapes again.

5 When the sheet of paper is completely dry, gently peel the templates away to reveal a colourful Christmas design. Place it face down on your work surface.

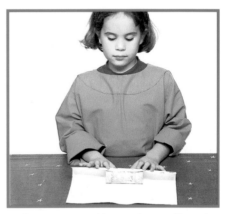

6 Brush glue all over the cardboard tube. Place it halfway along one edge of the sheet of paper. Carefully roll the paper around the tube. Glue the edge down.

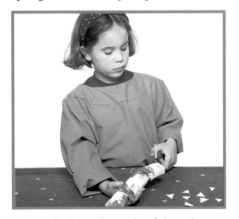

7 Feel where the ends of the tube are and pinch in the paper there. Finally, cut triangles from the ends of the paper and add ribbons.

The ideal table decoration for a Christmas party.

Painted Stones Caterpillar

If you are unable to get to the seaside to collect the pebbles, make some from self-hardening clay which can be bought in craft and hobby shops. When you have painted the pebbles with pictures or numbers, you will have hours of fun with them. Joshua is being clever with his pebbles by painting a caterpillar on one side and numbers and mathematical signs on the other, so that he can practise his sums and see how brainy he is.

Painting tips

You will find it easier to paint half of all the stones, then go back and finish them off. In this way, you won't be trying to hold an area of stone that is already wet.

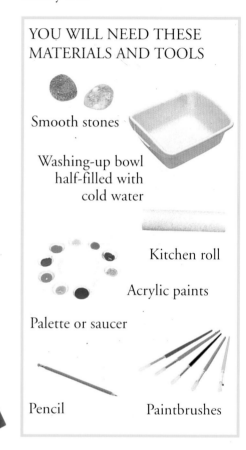

YOU WILL NEED THESE MATERIALS AND TOOLS

Smooth stones

Washing-up bowl half-filled with cold water

Kitchen roll

Acrylic paints

Palette or saucer

Pencil

Paintbrushes

50

1 Wash the stones in the washing-up bowl and dry them well with kitchen roll. Use as many as you like.

2 Paint the stones. Try to make each one a different colour. Leave them on your work surface until they are completely dry.

3 Arrange the stones in a long line with the biggest at one end and the smallest at the other. Draw a caterpillar design on them.

4 Paint the caterpillar's body using different colours. Use black, brown or another dark colour for its feet.

5 Decorate each part of its body with different coloured spots. You can vary the size of the spots too.

6 Either use a new set of painted stones, or wait until the caterpillar is dry and turn the stones over. Paint in some figures and mathematical symbols.

7 Impress your family and friends by showing them how clever you are.

None of your papers will blow away when the caterpillar is weighing them down.

Butterfly Blottography Box

Blottography prints are easy to do and the results are always an exciting surprise. This technique is at least 100 years old. Alice is using her prints to brighten up a storage box, but you could also stick a blottography shape to a tray and varnish over it – ask a grown-up to help with this.

Blottography technique
Be sure to use a large piece of paper for your prints so that paint doesn't ooze out over everything and make a mess.

YOU WILL NEED THESE MATERIALS AND TOOLS

White cartridge paper

Acrylic or poster paints

Palette or saucer

Paintbrushes

Scissors

Shoebox or other cardboard box

PVA glue and a spreader

1 Make sure that your sheet of paper is longer than it is wide. Fold it in half lengthways.

2 Open up the paper and dab generous spots of paint on one side only. Use as many different colours as you like, but don't get it *too* runny.

3 Fold the paper in half once again, bringing the dry side over on to the wet side. Carefully smooth it down with your hand.

4 Open up the paper and admire the colourful, symmetrical pattern you have created on both sides of the paper. Leave it to dry thoroughly.

5 Make some more patterns of different sizes and using different colour combinations in the same way. Try using all pale colours or all dark. Cut them out when they are dry.

A colourful way of storing your odds and ends.

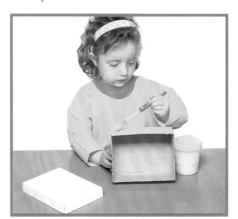

6 Paint the cardboard box inside and out. If you are using a shoe-box, or any other box that was coloured to start with, you will find it easier to cover the existing colour if you use acrylic paint. Poster paint is fine if your box is white to start with.

7 When the box is completely dry, glue your patterns to the box.

Vegetable-print T-shirts

Sasha is using different colours and all sorts of vegetables on a white T-shirt. If you don't want to make an all-over design, you could print just in the centre of the shirt. For a more intricate design, use smaller vegetables such as tiny onions cut in half, or a baby carrot. Use different sizes of mushroom too.

Design rules
If you are not sure about a design, print it on paper first to get a good idea of how it will look when it is on the T-shirt. Once it is on the T-shirt it will be difficult to remove or change.

YOU WILL NEED THESE MATERIALS AND TOOLS

Selection of vegetables

Chopping board

Kitchen knife

Plain T-shirt – white for preference

Newspaper

Fabric paints

Paintbrushes

1 Choose vegetables that will make interesting prints of different sizes, such as a stick of celery (semi-circle), carrot (circle), pepper (crinkly circle), mushroom and leek.

2 Ask a grown-up to cut up the vegetables for you. Make sure that they cut round the pepper – you don't want a strip – and leave the stalk on the mushroom slice.

3 Lay the T-shirt flat and front side up on your work surface. Put some newspapers inside so that your design does not go through to the back of the T-shirt.

4 Paint the edge of the pepper with fabric paint. Make sure that the edge is covered with paint but don't get it too wet or it might smudge.

5 Print the pepper on to the T-shirt. Try to hold it still while it is in contact with the shirt so that the edges don't blur. You may need to repaint it between prints.

6 Paint the end of the carrot with fabric paint and use it to print in the centre of and all around the pepper prints. Try not to print over another print as the colours may run.

7 Use all the other vegetables in the same way, choosing different colours and building up an interesting design. Leave the T-shirt to dry.

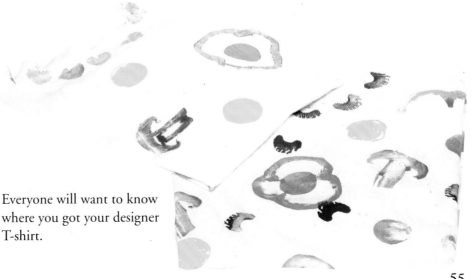

Everyone will want to know where you got your designer T-shirt.

Spotty Dog-bone Picture Frame

Frame a picture of your pet with one of these fun frames. Nicholas is using a colourful photograph of his dog. Or you could frame your paintings and put on an exhibition of your works of art.

Framing

If you are making a frame for one of your favourite pictures then you will need to make sure that the hole in the middle of your frame is cut to the right size. Measure your picture before you begin and then make the hole slightly smaller than this. If the hole is too big the backing sheet will show through.

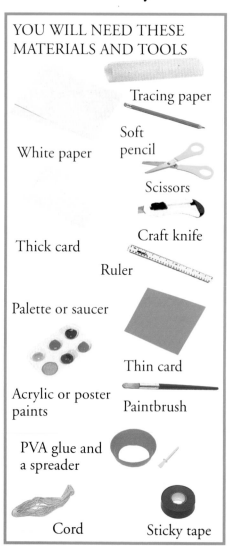

YOU WILL NEED THESE
MATERIALS AND TOOLS

Tracing paper

White paper

Soft pencil

Scissors

Craft knife

Thick card

Ruler

Palette or saucer

Thin card

Acrylic or poster paints

Paintbrush

PVA glue and a spreader

Cord

Sticky tape

1 Using a soft pencil, trace the dog-bone template from the beginning of the book on to white paper six times.

2 Cut out the dog bone shapes using the scissors. Take care as you cut round the curves so that you get six even-looking bones.

3 Paint each bone. When the background colour has dried, paint on some spots. Don't choose very bright colours for either the bones or spots.

4 Ask a grown-up to cut the card for the frame, and to cut out the centre. Cut a piece of thin card slightly larger than the hole in the centre of the frame.

5 Paint the frame a plain colour that will look attractive with your bones and with the photograph you intend to display in the frame. Leave it to dry.

6 Glue the bones on to the frame. Push out any air bubbles with your fingers. If you have used too much glue, let it dry then peel it off.

7 Stick a loop of cord to the top of the back of the frame. Then attach the backing card with tape, leaving the top free so that you can slip your photograph inside.

A special frame for a special photograph.

Bubble-printed Notebook

It is a good idea to do bubble printing as close to the kitchen sink as you can since you need lots of water and washing-up liquid to make fluffy bubbles. Don't lift a full bowl of water yourself – ask a grown-up to do it.

The secret of bubble printing is not to pour in too many colours at once. Remember you can always add more if you don't like the first sheet.

Food colouring

If you can't find coloured inks you could use food colourings instead. You may find there are not as many different colours and most of them will be paler than some inks but you will still get good results.

YOU WILL NEED THESE MATERIALS AND TOOLS

Washing-up bowl

Washing-up liquid

Coloured inks

White cartridge paper

Scissors

Newspaper

Notebook

PVA glue and a spreader

1 Squeeze a generous amount of washing-up liquid into the washing-up bowl.

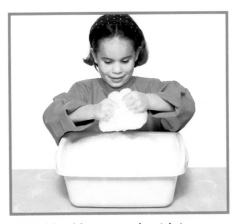

2 Add cold water and swish it around so that there are plenty of bubbles in the bowl.

3 Gradually dribble different coloured inks on to the surface of the bubbles.

4 Cut a piece of cartridge paper about the same size as the bowl. Gently lay the paper on the surface of the coloured bubbles.

5 Carefully remove the paper from the bowl and place it face up on sheets of newspaper to dry.

6 If the paper dries crinkly, flatten it by placing it in between some heavy books and leaving it overnight.

Decorate your notebooks, diary and address book with your individual bubble-printed papers.

7 Open the notebook and cut the paper, adding an extra 2.5 cm (1 in) all around. Cut across the corners and cut a V at the top and bottom of the spine. Glue the extra inside the cover.

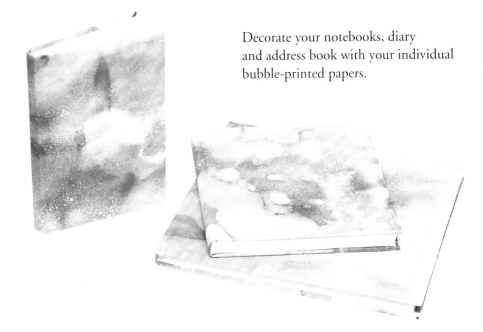

Finger-painted Flowers

These wild and colourful flowers brighten up any room and don't even need to be watered. The great thing about making your own flowers is that you can choose which colours you want them to be and if you paint the backs and fronts differently, you can turn them round when you get bored.

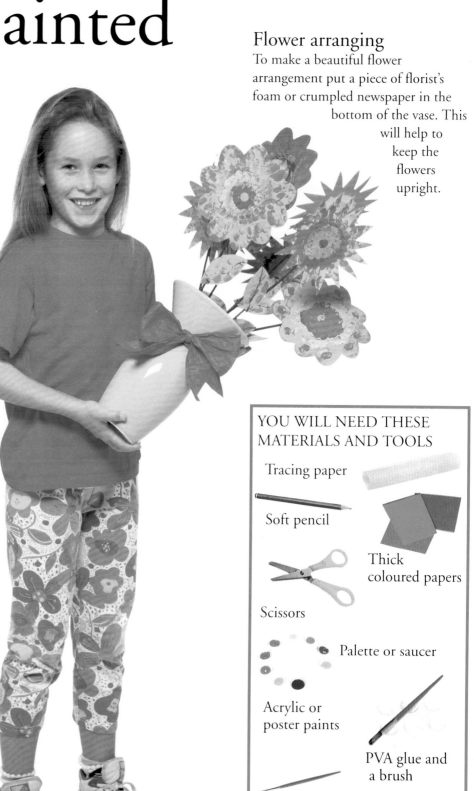

Flower arranging

To make a beautiful flower arrangement put a piece of florist's foam or crumpled newspaper in the bottom of the vase. This will help to keep the flowers upright.

YOU WILL NEED THESE MATERIALS AND TOOLS

Tracing paper

Soft pencil

Thick coloured papers

Scissors

Palette or saucer

Acrylic or poster paints

PVA glue and a brush

Thin paintbrush

Garden sticks

Sticky tape

1 Using a soft pencil, trace the flower, circle and leaf templates from the front of the book on to coloured paper.

2 Using the scissors, cut out the shapes. You will need two matching flower shapes, two circles and two leaf shapes for each flower.

3 Glue a circle of coloured paper on to the centre of each flower. Make sure that the flowers and circles are different colours.

4 Dip your fingers one at a time into the paint and then press them on to your flowers. Use a different finger for each colour. Cover the flowers with finger prints.

5 Leave the flowers to dry thoroughly while you make the leaves. Finger paint the leaf shapes with different green paints and paint a fine line of colour down the centre of each one to make the vein. Leave them to dry.

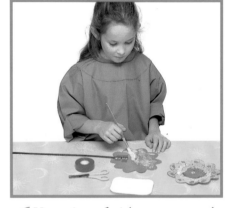

6 Use a piece of sticky tape to attach a garden stick to the back of a flower. Glue a matching flower on to the back and gently press it down to make sure that it sticks.

7 Attach the back of one leaf to the garden stick with sticky tape and glue a matching leaf to the back of it.

Everlasting flowers brighten up the dullest day

61

Wooden-spoon Puppets

Tania and Joshua are having fun painting their puppets. Create your own theatre characters on wooden spoons then put on a show to impress the grown-ups. Hide behind the sofa and use its back as the stage. Try to give all the characters different voices too.

Drying tip

Stand the spoons in a jam jar while the wet heads dry. To dry the handles, stand the heads in a big lump of modelling clay.

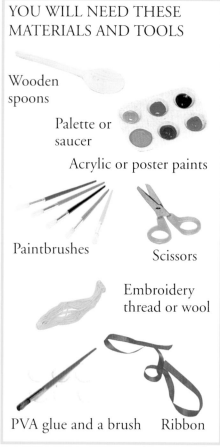

YOU WILL NEED THESE MATERIALS AND TOOLS

Wooden spoons

Palette or saucer

Acrylic or poster paints

Paintbrushes

Scissors

Embroidery thread or wool

PVA glue and a brush   Ribbon

1 Paint the head of the spoon and leave it to dry.

2 Paint the handle of the spoon using a different colour and leave it to dry.

3 Decorate the handle with spots, stripes, collar, buttons or a bow tie.

4 Paint a face on to the head of the spoon and leave to dry. If you are making a man puppet, paint on some hair or, if you prefer, leave him bald.

5 If you are making a lady, cut about 15 strands of embroidery thread all the same length. Tie a shorter piece around the middle of them to keep them together.

6 Glue the hair on to the top of the lady's head and leave it to dry. Try not to use too much glue. If you do, let it dry, then peel off the excess with your fingers.

Make your own theatre and impress your friends with your own plays.

7 Tie the ribbon into a bow and glue it on to the hair.

Wax-resist Badges

Add a personal touch to a favourite outfit with a badge made with the magical technique of wax resist. Alice is using wax crayons, which give a colourful result, but the technique also works in black and white if you use a candle to draw your design. Remember that as your badge is made out of card, you can't wear it outside in the rain.

Age badges

A variation on this idea is to make an age badge for you or a friend, or your little brother or sister. Vary the colours to suit the personality of the wearer.

YOU WILL NEED THESE MATERIALS AND TOOLS

Wax crayons

White card

Dark coloured poster paint

Paintbrush

Scissors

Sticky tape

Safety pins

1 Collect together all the materials you will need for the project before you begin.

2 Draw a flowerpot shape on to the card with wax crayons. The brighter the colours, the more attractive the finished badge will be.

3 Add a cactus in a different colour, then decorate the pot and cactus using as many colours as you like.

4 Paint over your wax drawing with poster paint. Don't worry about the edges too much as you are going to cut out the picture later.

5 When the paint is completely dry, you should still be able to see your wax drawing. Cut around the edge of the cactus and flowerpot.

6 Turn the badge over. Cut a small piece of sticky tape and use it to attach the safety pin to the middle of the badge.

It's obvious who is on your team with these colourful badges.

Flowery Glass

These jolly flowers will liven up any glass frame. You could also use lots of smaller flower stickers to decorate a jam jar to use as a pencil pot or flower vase.

Aaron is decorating a frame but you can stick the flowers on the inside of a real window as in step 7.

Handy hints

Plastic film is quite difficult to smooth down without getting air bubbles trapped. The trick is to work slowly, peeling off a bit of backing and smoothing as you go.

YOU WILL NEED THESE MATERIALS AND TOOLS

Plastic film

Scissors

Sticky tape

Palette or saucer

Acrylic paints

Paintbrushes

1 Cut two pieces of plastic film the same size. Stick the corners of one piece to your work surface with sticky tape. Do not remove the backing.

2 Paint the centre of a flower on to the centre of one piece of the film. Use a bright colour such as red, purple or yellow.

3 Using a different colour, paint five petals around the centre of the flower. Take care not to smudge the centre as you paint.

4 Decorate the flower with spots of a different, bright colour. Leave the flower to dry completely.

5 Take the second piece of film and carefully peel away the film's backing. Stick it over the flower. Work slowly, smoothing out any air bubbles with your fingers as you go.

6 If you get an air bubble, prick it with the point of a needle and smooth it out, then carefully cut around the flower.

7 Peel off the backing and stick the flower to the inside of your window.

Have year-round flowers on your bedroom window.

Flick-painted Starscape

This is a messy project so be sure to cover your work surface with lots of newspaper or scrap paper, or, if the weather is fine, do your flick painting outside. You can use any size of box for the planet story. The planet and rocket will move if you blow them or put the box by an open window.

If you want to make the inside of the box sparkle, add some glitter or cut out star shapes from kitchen foil and scatter them around the box.

Large-scale scene

A shoebox was used for this project but if you want to make a really big scene, get a box from the supermarket that had apples or oranges in it. Remember to make more than one of each mobile if you are using a big box.

YOU WILL NEED THESE MATERIALS AND TOOLS

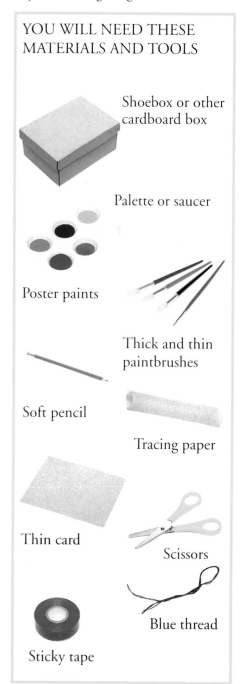

Shoebox or other cardboard box

Palette or saucer

Poster paints

Thick and thin paintbrushes

Soft pencil

Tracing paper

Thin card

Scissors

Blue thread

Sticky tape

1 Paint the shoebox inside and out using blue paint. You don't need the lid so don't bother with that. Leave the box to dry, then stand it on a wipe-clean surface, inside a cardboard box, or on a surface covered with newspaper.

2 Dip a medium-sized paintbrush in one of your pots of poster paint and flick the paint into the box. For fine splatters, tap the brush handle on the edge of the box. Repeat this with the different coloured paints.

3 Leave the box to dry thoroughly while you make the mobiles and decorations. Using a soft pencil, trace the star, planet and rocket templates from the beginning of the book on to pieces of card.

4 Cut out the shapes. If your box is large, you will need more than one of each. You will also need some stars for the outside of the box.

5 Cover your work surface with scrap paper, then paint each shape. Choose yellow, gold or silver for the stars and bright colours for the planet and rocket.

6 Use a piece of sticky tape to attach a length of blue thread to the shapes to hang inside the box. Glue some of the stars to the top and sides of the box.

7 Use sticky tape to attach the rocket and planet to the roof of the box.

Your own space scene will amaze your friends.

Marbled Pencils and Pencil Pot

The exciting thing about marbled papers is that each sheet is different and unique. Marbling is simple to do, but always ask a grown-up to mix the oil paint as you must not get turpentine near your eyes or mouth. You can buy ready-mixed marbling colours from craft or hobby shops.

Marbling technique

The secret of good marbling is not to pour too much paint into the water at once. You can always add more after you have made one sheet of paper if you think it is too pale.

YOU WILL NEED THESE MATERIALS AND TOOLS

Oil paints

Plastic cups

Newspaper

White spirit or turpentine

Washing-up bowl half-filled with cold water

Scissors

Small stick, such as a garden stick or an old paintbrush

Small carton

Cartridge paper or lining paper

PVA glue and a brush

Pencils

1 Squeeze a blob of about five different paints into separate plastic cups and ask a grown-up to add a small amount of turpentine. Mix well.

2 Cover your work surface with newspaper. Place the washing-up bowl on the work surface. Gradually pour the oil paints into the water.

3 Mix the paints around to make interesting patterns. Make sure that you haven't got a big blob of one colour completely unmixed.

4 Cut a piece of paper about the same size as the washing-up bowl and gently place it on the surface of the patterned water.

5 Remove the paper carefully and place it face up on a flat surface covered with newspaper. Try making different papers, experimenting with different colours and patterns.

6 When your papers are completely dry, use one to cover the carton. Cut it to shape, then glue it down. Leave some paper at the top to glue down inside the box.

7 Cover some pencils with your marbled paper so they match your pencil holder.

Cheer up homework time with your unique pencils and pot.

71

Modelling Fun

Thomasina Smith

Introduction

Modelling is not just about making sculptures of animals or people, it is also about creating useful things like pots and plates. Even jewellery can be fashioned from modelling material and then decorated. In ancient cultures, nearly everything needed for cooking or for serving food was made from clay. The clay was then baked to make it hard. The ancient Greeks used clay to make beautiful pots, called urns, in which they collected water and stored food. Many of these pots were decorated with patterns or pictures and then painted.

Types of modelling materials

In Modelling Fun, we use several different types of modelling material. There are projects that use a material that hardens when baked in the oven, a special drying material that hardens without baking, and a plastic type that remains soft so that it can be used over and over again.

There are also projects made with salt dough. This can be made at home by using the recipe that follows. All the other types of modelling materials can be bought in toy, craft or hobby shops.

Always store your modelling materials in sealed plastic bags or airtight containers. This will keep them clean and ready for future use. Drying modelling material will harden if it is left out in the open air.

What you can make

Your friends will be astounded when they see the weird and wonderful things you have made using the projects in Modelling Fun. There is a Grinning Cat, a Snappy Crocodile and a Coiled Pot and Plate. There is also a pirate's Treasure Chest and a Space Rocket. The project that will doubly impress your friends is the Spotty Clock. Not only does its salt dough clock face look terrific, but it tells the time!

After making a few of the models shown here, why not design some of your own? You could create some more characters like Wonder Boy and write a play about their adventures. Once you have learned the knack of making animals, you could create your own miniature wildlife park or farmyard. There is no end to the amount of crafty modelling fun you can have.

Safety

There are a few rules to follow when preparing and baking your models.

1. To cut a piece of modelling material, use a butter knife or the bladed end of a plastic modelling tool. Modelling materials are soft – there is no need for sharp cutting utensils.

2. Always ask an adult to turn on the oven and set the temperature. An adult should supervise placing the baking tray into the oven and removing it. When doing these things and transferring the baked items to a cooling rack, always wear a pair of oven gloves. Do not touch the baked items until they have had time to cool down.

3. Keep hot baking trays and modelling materials out of reach of young children.

Materials and equipment

Acrylic paint This is a water-based paint that comes in a range of vibrant colours.

Baking modelling material This material hardens when it is baked in an oven. It comes in a range of colours. Always read the instructions on the packet.

Baking tray You will need a baking tray when using baking modelling material.

Biscuit cutters These are used to cut interesting shapes from modelling material. Use either plastic or metal ones.

Chopping board Use a plastic chopping board to protect tabletops when modelling. Wash thoroughly after use.

Cooling rack After the salt dough has baked in the oven, place it on a cooling rack to cool before painting.

Drying modelling material This white or terracotta modelling material will harden in about 24 hours without baking. Always read the instructions on the packet.

Fine sandpaper Before the baked salt dough is painted, rough edges are smoothed by rubbing sandpaper over them.

Modelling tool The most useful modelling tool has one pointy end and one flat end. This tool can be used for carving and sculpting.

Oven gloves These must be worn when removing a baking tray from the oven and when handling hot salt dough models.

Parchment paper This prevents the salt dough sticking to the baking tray when it is baking.

Plastic modelling material This inexpensive and reusable material comes in lots of bright colours. It does not harden, so the models are less permanent.

PVA glue This is strong glue for joining surfaces but it can also be mixed with water to make a varnish for your models.

Rolling pin This is for rolling salt dough flat. Before using, dust the rolling pin with flour to stop the dough sticking.

Tall, thick glass Use a thick glass for rolling out baking, drying or plastic modelling material. Do not use a wooden rolling pin – these materials will stick to it.

Varnish If you do not want to make a varnish with PVA glue, you can buy ready-made varnish from art and craft shops.

Acrylic paints

Drying modelling material

Modelling tool

Masking tape

Cardboard and coloured card

Baking tray

Tall, thick glass

Chopping board

Paintbrush

PVA glue

Plastic modelling material

Fine sandpaper

Biscuit cutters

Baking modelling material

Plastic bags

Oven gloves

Varnish

Parchment paper

Rolling pin

Cooling rack

75

Basic Techniques

These basic techniques apply to baking, drying and plastic modelling materials.

To soften modelling material, hold it in your hands. Their warmth will soften it and make it easy to model.

To roll out modelling material, apply even pressure and use a thick glass to get a smooth surface of the right thickness.

Shaping materials

To shape modelling materials you can use your hands to make round or oval balls, and snakes and sausages. The secret to modelling with your hands is to be patient and to mould the material gently. If you press too firmly, ball shapes will become blobs and snakes will be uneven. To make textures, smooth joins or to cut modelling materials, it is best to use a modelling tool. For small, detail work like adding features to a face, a cocktail stick is perfect. You can also shape modelling material by moulding it on to a plate or around a cup.

To make snake and sausage shapes, roll the modelling material back and forth under the palms of your hands and fingers. Move your hands along the material to make it even.

To make a round ball, gently roll a piece of modelling material between your flattened palms. Cut the ball in half with a modelling tool or butter knife to make dome shapes.

Attaching limbs

One way of securely fixing limbs to a body is to score lots of fine lines on both pieces. Press the pieces together and smooth the join using a modelling tool.

An alternative method is to make a hole in the body with the thin end of a modelling tool. Shape the end of the limb into a point and push it into the hole firmly.

Keeping colours separate

To stop plastic modelling material colours being mixed together, tape sheets of white paper on to your work surface or chopping board. Roll or model only one colour of material on each sheet. After finishing a model, put the paper aside and use it the next time you use the same colour.

How to Make Salt Dough

For some of the projects you need to make a quantity of salt dough.

YOU WILL NEED THESE MATERIALS AND TOOLS

300g (11 oz) salt

300g (11 oz) flour

30ml (2 tbsp) vegetable oil

200ml (7 fl oz) water

Mixing bowl

Scales

Wooden spoon

Measuring jug

Plastic bag

1 Use the scales to weigh the correct amount of flour and salt. Put the flour and salt in the bowl. Mix them together using the wooden spoon.

2 Measure 200ml (7 fl oz) of water in a measuring jug. Pour the water gradually over the flour and salt and mix well.

3 Pour the oil over the mixture and mix it in well. When all the oil has been absorbed, remove the dough from the bowl and place on a clean surface that has been sprinkled with flour.

4 Knead the dough with your hands until it is firm, then put it in a plastic bag or wrap it in plastic food wrap. Place the dough in the refrigerator for 30 minutes before you use it.

Handy hint

If you do not use all the salt dough you have made, store it in an airtight container or a plastic bag and put it in the refrigerator. When you want to use it again, simply sprinkle it with flour and knead it. This will soften the salt dough and make it easy to work with.

Remember that models made with salt dough will be fragile, so handle them with care.

Space Rocket

This rocket is made using a rocket-shaped cardboard base covered with colourful plastic modelling material. Not only does this method make the model stronger, it means that you can be more inventive when you design your own deep-Space explorer.

YOU WILL NEED THESE MATERIALS AND TOOLS

Coloured pencil

Thick cardboard

Scissors

Ruler

Masking tape

Chopping board

Modelling tool

Tall, thick glass

Plastic modelling material (white, black, purple, green, orange, yellow)

'Mission control to Space Rocket commander, are you ready for blast off? We are starting countdown.'

1 On a piece of thick cardboard, use the pencil to draw two tongue-like shapes 20cm x 8cm (8in x 3in). On one of the shapes mark a 3mm (1/16in) wide slit, as shown. On the other, draw semi-circular fins on either side.

2 Cut out both pieces and the slit. Slot the finned piece into the slit so that the rocket will stand upright. If the model leans to one side, trim the base to straighten it. Fasten the joins with masking tape.

3 Roll out pieces of plastic modelling material in different colours. Mould these firmly on to the card base, pinching the joins together securely. Use the modelling tool to trim the edges and draw markings.

4 When the rocket is covered with modelling material, press on flattened balls of modelling material to make windows and rivets.

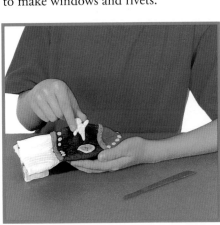

5 Mould an astronaut from white material. Make a hole in a window and press the astronaut into the hole.

Once you have constructed your first Space Rocket, you can go on to design a whole fleet of rockets, Space labs or alien Space ships. It is best not to make the cardboard base too large because the amount of modelling material needed to cover it will keep your craft Earthbound.

Spotty Clock

Watch time tick by on this Spotty Clock. The only special items you require to make this working clock are a pair of clock hands and clock workings. These can be bought in specialist hobby and craft shops. Check which size battery is required and read the assembly instructions for the kit carefully.

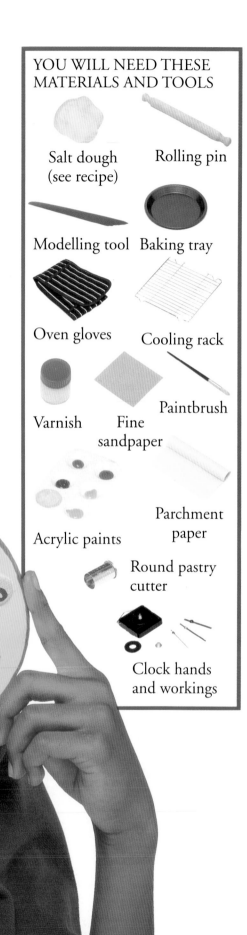

YOU WILL NEED THESE MATERIALS AND TOOLS

Salt dough (see recipe)

Rolling pin

Modelling tool

Baking tray

Oven gloves

Cooling rack

Varnish

Fine sandpaper

Paintbrush

Acrylic paints

Parchment paper

Round pastry cutter

Clock hands and workings

1 Roll out a piece of salt dough to 1cm (¹/₂in) thick. Place a plate on the dough and cut round it. Find the centre of the circle and make a small hole. Make sure the clock workings will go through this hole.

2 Roll out another piece of salt dough to about 5mm (¹/₄in) thick and cut out 12 circles of dough with the round pastry cutter. Stick four circles of dough on to the clock face with a dab of water to mark 12, 3, 6 and 9. Use the remaining circles to decorate the clock face. Bake the clock face on a baking tray lined with parchment paper for about five hours at 120°C/250°F/Gas ½.

3 Ask an adult to remove the hardened salt dough from the oven with oven gloves and place it on a cooling rack. When cool, smooth the edge of the clock face with sandpaper. Paint the clock face a light colour before painting the circles in contrasting colours. It is good idea to paint the circles for 12, 3, 6 and 9 in the same colour. Paint a line around the edge of the clock face.

4 Mark the four points of the clock face by painting on the numbers. When dry, apply a coat of varnish. Attach the clock hands and workings following the instructions on the kit.

This is just one way of decorating the clock face. You may like to use stars, squares, diamonds, hearts or flower shapes. These shapes and many more can be made with fancy biscuit cutters. It is important that the shapes are not too large or too thick. If they are too thick, the hands will not be able to move around the clock face.

Snappy Crocodile

This fantastic crocodile is made from a special modelling clay that hardens when baked in the oven. This means that Snappy will be flashing its fangs at passers-by for years to come. Just like a real crocodile, Snappy has pointy teeth and stays cool by keeping its mouth open.

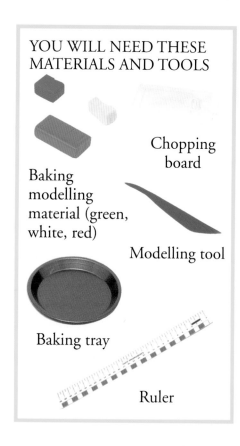

YOU WILL NEED THESE MATERIALS AND TOOLS

Chopping board

Baking modelling material (green, white, red)

Modelling tool

Baking tray

Ruler

1 Roll one sausage 15cm (6in) long, another 6cm (2½in) long and four more 5cm (2in) long. Roll two balls for the eyes. Shape the two large sausages to make Snappy's body and upper jaw.

2 Press the jaw and legs into position. Bend the back legs to look like those of a real crocodile. Fold the front legs so that they are thicker at the top. Smooth the joins with your fingers.

3 Press a ball of white material on to each of the small green balls. Press a little red material on top to complete the eyes. Position the eyes to cover the join between the jaw and body.

4 Cut four rectangular strips of white modelling material. Carefully carve small triangles from the strips to make pointed and jagged teeth. Position them neatly along Snappy's jaws. Press them firmly into position.

5 Use the modelling tool to mark scales on the crocodile's back. Place your masterpiece on a baking tray. Ask an adult to put it in the oven and to bake it according to the instructions on the packet.

Toothy reminder

Snappy's brilliant white teeth could act as a reminder for you to clean your teeth. To transform Snappy into the most ferocious toothbrush holder in the world, just make sure that when modelling its mouth the opening is wide enough to fit a toothbrush.

Did you know that crocodiles can grow to a length of 6m (20ft)? But do not try to make a life-size Snappy model because it will never fit in the oven!

Coiled Plate

This plate is for decoration only! Remember to use an ovenproof plate for the mould.

1 Divide the dough into three balls. Make a well in the centre of each ball and add three drops of food colouring to each. Each ball will be a different colour. Knead them on a floured surface to spread the colouring evenly. Lightly oil the ovenproof plate.

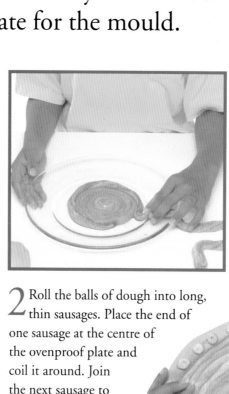

2 Roll the balls of dough into long, thin sausages. Place the end of one sausage at the centre of the ovenproof plate and coil it around. Join the next sausage to the end of the first piece and continue coiling. Do the same with the remaining sausage.

3 Decorate the edge and centre of the plate with small balls of coloured dough. Bake the plate in the oven for six hours at 120°C/ 250°F/Gas ½. Ask an adult to remove the hardened salt dough from the oven with oven gloves and transfer to a cooling rack.

When cool, give your Coiled Plate a shiny finish by applying a coat of varnish.

Snake Pot

This little storage pot looks like a sleeping snake curled around on itself.

YOU WILL NEED THESE MATERIALS AND TOOLS

White drying modelling material

PVA glue

Chopping board

Acrylic paints

Paintbrush

Modelling tool

1 Cut three pieces of drying modelling material and roll each into a snake. Make each one as long as possible but not too thin. Tightly coil one of the snakes into a flat circle. This will be the base of the pot. If there are any gaps, gently press them together. Bind the joins with the modelling tool.

2 Build the walls of the pot by coiling a snake on top of the outer edge of the base. Smooth the ridges on the inside of the pot. Continue coiling with the second snake. When you have finished, shape the end to make the snake's face. Use the modelling tool to carve a pattern around the edge.

Handy hint

If you want to make a larger coil pot to use as a pencil holder, roll the snakes a little thicker. If you need more snakes to complete your pot, bind the snakes together and keep coiling.

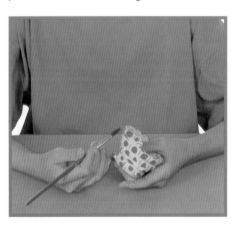

3 Allow the pot to dry for about 12 hours on each side before painting it yellow with red spots. To finish, apply a varnish made of 8 parts PVA glue and 1 part water.

The Snake Pot is the perfect place to store small treasures or even pocket money. No one would dare touch it for fear of disturbing the sleeping snake!

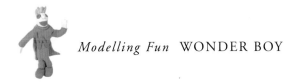

Wonder Boy

Like all great superheroes, Wonder Boy wears a dashing cape and has superhuman powers. You could build a whole story world about Wonder Boy's thrilling adventures from modelling material. Your hero could save a city of skyscrapers from the rampages of monsters and dinosaurs!

YOU WILL NEED THESE
MATERIALS AND TOOLS

Modelling tool

Chopping
board

Plastic modelling material
(green, orange, white,
red, yellow)

1 Roll out four small sausages and one large sausage from green modelling material. The large sausage will be the superhero's body, so it should be narrow at the top and wide at the bottom.

2 Firmly press the four small sausages on to the body to make the legs and arms of Wonder Boy. Use your fingers to carefully bind and smooth the joins. Make sure that your model can stand.

3 Roll out orange modelling material and shape it to make a cloak. Shape two white balls to make fists, and two red balls to make a pair of shoes. Press the pieces into position and decorate.

4 To make the face, roll a ball of white material. Use scraps of modelling material to make the eyes, mouth and nose. Carve a piece of yellow material for the hair and press it into position.

5 Roll a thin, short sausage of green material, shape it into a small circle and position it where the head will go. Press the head firmly on to the body and smooth the join. Lay Wonder Boy gently on to his back.

If you want to give your superhero a different name, do not forget to alter the letter on the model's chest. In place of a letter, you can use a star, lightning flash or other symbol.

6 Roll out a snake of red material. Press it on to Wonder Boy's chest in the shape of the letter 'W'.

Family of Pigs

These three little pigs would make lovely ornaments for a shelf or window ledge. They would be the perfect gift for someone who collects models of pigs. Sows can have up to ten piglets in a litter, so make as many as you like!

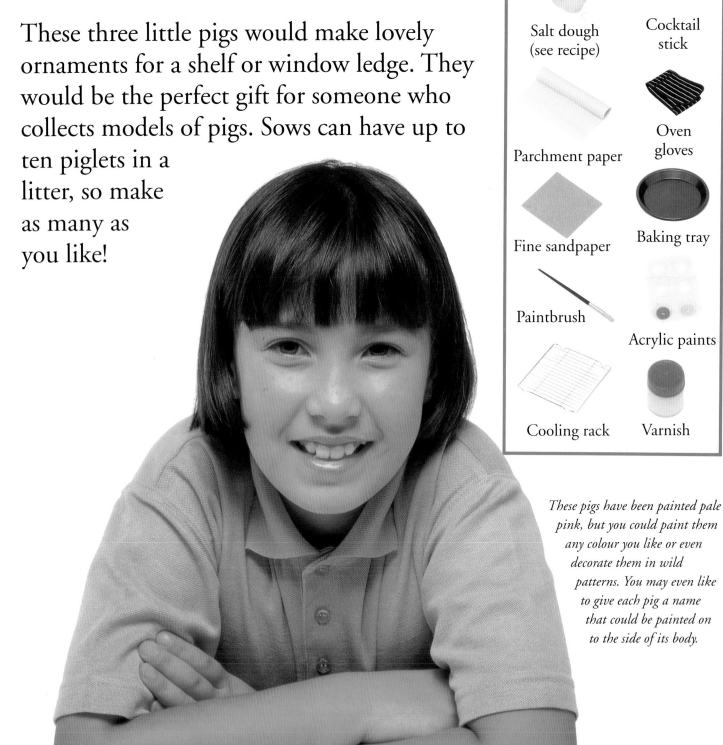

YOU WILL NEED THESE MATERIALS AND TOOLS

Salt dough (see recipe)

Cocktail stick

Parchment paper

Oven gloves

Fine sandpaper

Baking tray

Paintbrush

Acrylic paints

Cooling rack

Varnish

These pigs have been painted pale pink, but you could paint them any colour you like or even decorate them in wild patterns. You may even like to give each pig a name that could be painted on to the side of its body.

1 Roll pieces of dough to make three oval shapes of different sizes. Shape one end of each oval into a pig's face and use a cocktail stick to mark eyes and nostrils. Attach two small triangles of dough on to each head for the ears.

2 Roll a small piece of salt dough into a long strip for each pig's tail and stick one on to the back of each pig with a dab of water. Gently bend it into a coil shape. Place the pigs on a baking tray lined with parchment paper.

3 Form 12 stumpy, round legs from small balls of salt dough. Try to make the legs the same size. Place them on the baking tray with the pigs' bodies. Ask an adult to bake them in the oven for five hours at 120°C/250°F/Gas ½.

⚠ SAFETY

Always ask an adult to help you set the oven temperature. Wear oven gloves when placing the baking tray in the oven and when removing it. A pair of tongs or an egg slice will make it easy and safe to transfer hot items from the baking tray on to the cooling rack. Allow plenty of time for your models to cool.

4 When cool, join four legs on to each body with salt dough and a dab of water. Place the pigs back in the oven at the same temperature for two hours.

5 Allow the finished pigs to cool on a rack before smoothing any rough parts with sandpaper. To finish, paint and varnish your Family of Pigs.

Treasure Chest

This treasure chest is a great place to keep small and precious things. It is made of drying modelling material that slowly hardens when left in the air. The skull and crossbones on the front is the traditional sign of a pirate ship.

Handy hint

Roll out the modelling material for the base and sides of the chest to about 5mm (¼in) in thickness. If the material is rolled too thinly, the sides of the chest may collapse.

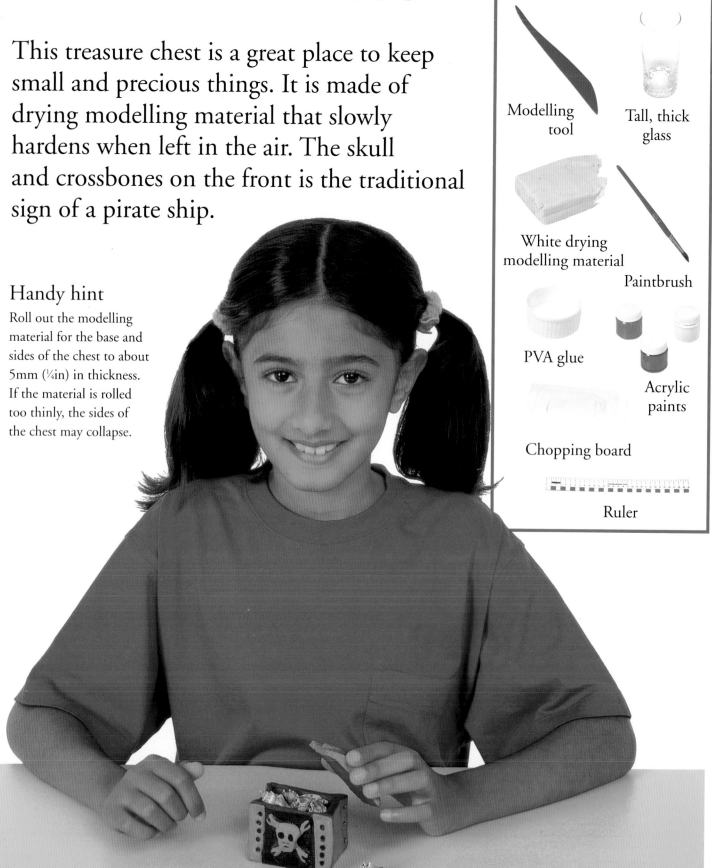

YOU WILL NEED THESE MATERIALS AND TOOLS

Modelling tool

Tall, thick glass

White drying modelling material

Paintbrush

PVA glue

Acrylic paints

Chopping board

Ruler

1 Roll out the material. Cut out two sides and a base each 6cm x 4cm (2½in x 1½in), and two more sides each 4cm x 4cm (1½in x 1½in). Cut a strip 8cm (3in) long for the lid strap.

2 Score around the sides of the base with the modelling tool. Position the first side and smooth the inside join. Position the remaining sides and smooth the inside joins.

3 When all the sides are in place, smooth the outside edges with the tool. Use the point of the tool to make dots in the modelling material to create the effect of studs.

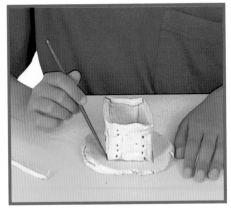

4 Roll out another piece of modelling material and place the chest on it. Cut around the chest so that the rectangle for the lid will be exactly the same size as the base of the chest.

5 Decorate the lid and fix the strap on to the lid. Place the lid on the chest. Decorate the chest with a skull and crossbones cut from modelling material. Allow the chest to dry for 24 hours.

6 When the chest is dry and hard, paint it inside and outside with acrylic paints. Allow the paint to dry before applying a coat of varnish made from 8 parts PVA glue to 1 part water.

The Treasure Chest would make a wonderful birthday or Christmas gift for a friend if filled with chocolate coins wrapped in gold foil. If you want to use your Treasure Chest to store small, fragile valuables, line the treasure chest with cotton wool.

Grinning Cat

This grinning cat looks very pleased with itself. You can almost hear it purring! This model is very simple to make because the cat's legs are curled tightly under its body. Do not make the tail too thin or it will break.

YOU WILL NEED THESE MATERIALS AND TOOLS

Modelling tool

White drying modelling material

Acrylic paints

PVA glue

Paintbrush

1 Roll a ball of white drying modelling material between your palms to make the head. Then roll a thick sausage 6cm (2¹/₂in) long and 2¹/₂cm (1in) wide for the cat's sleek body.

2 To fix the head on to the body, score the bottom of the head with the modelling tool and press the head firmly on to the body. Smooth the join with your fingers.

3 Cut and shape two pieces of modelling material to make the front paws. Press them into position. Make a tail and press it on to the body. Curl the tail around the body.

4 Flatten a small piece of modelling material with the palm of the your hand. Use the blade of the modelling tool to cut out two small triangles for the cat's ears.

5 Use the modelling tool to carve the features of the cat. You might want to practise this using a piece of leftover material. Allow the cat to dry for about 12 hours before starting to paint it.

6 Carefully paint the cat and use only the very boldest colours. Allow the paint to dry thoroughly before applying a varnish made of 8 parts PVA glue and 1 part water.

Paperweight Cat

Because Grinning Cat does little more all day than sit around looking pleased with itself, it would make a great paperweight. A paperweight stops sheets of paper from being blown around and lost. To make Paperweight Cat, all you have to do is make a larger and therefore heavier model. You will need to allow 24 hours for drying before painting.

Index

Acknowledgements

The publishers would like to thank the following children for appearing in the books in this series, and of course their parents:
Nana Addae, Richard Addae, Mohammed Adil Ali Ahmed, Josie and Lawrence Ainscombe, Clive Allen, Deborah Amoah, Charlie Anderson, Lauren Andrews, Rosie Anness, Michael Apeagyei, Tania Steve Aristizabal, Joshua Ashford, Emily Askew, Rula Awad, Nadia el-Ayadi, Joshua Ayshford, Nichola Barnard, Venetia Barrett, Jason Bear, Michael Bewley, Gurjit Kaur Bilkhu, Vikramjit Singh Bilkhu, Maria Bloodworth, Leah Bone, Catherine Brown, Chris Brown, Christopher Brown, Cerys Brunsdon, William Carabine, Daniel Carlow, Kristina Chase, Chan Chuvinh, Ngan Chuvinh, Alexander Clare, Rebecca Clee, Emma Cotton, Charlie Coulson, Brooke Crane, Charley Crittenden, Lawrence Defraitus, Dean Denning, Vicky Dummigan, Kimberley Durrance, Holly Everett, Alaba Fashina, Benjamin Ferguson, Terri Ferguson, Aimee Fermor, Kirsty and Rebecca Fraser, Fiona Fulton, Nicola Game, George Georgiev, Alice Granville, Lana Green, Liam and Lorenzo Green, Sophia Groome, Alexandra and Oliver Hall, Reece Harle, Laura Harris-Stewart, Jonathan Headon, Dominic Henry, Edward and Thomas Hogarth, Lauren Celeste Hooper, Mitzi Johanna Hooper, Sasha Howarth, Briony Irwin, Kayode Irwin, Gerald Ishiekwene, Saadia Jacobs, Stella-Rae James, Isha Janneh, Jade Jeffries, Aribibia Johnson, Rean Johnson, Reece Johnson, Carl Keating, Karina Kelly, Sarah Kenna, Camille Kenny-Ryder, Lee Knight, Nicola Kreinczes, Kevin Lake, Victoria Lebedeva, Barry Lee, Kirsty Lee, Isaac John Lewis, Nicholas Lie, Sophie, Alex and Otis Lindblom-Smith, Chloe Lipton, Scott Longstaff, Ephram Lovemore, Claire McCarthy, Erin McCarthy, Jock Maitland, Gabriella and Izabella Malewska, Ilaira and Joshua Mallalieu, Elouisa Markham, Alexander Martin-Simons, Laura Masters, Hou Mau, Trevor Meechan, Mickey Melaku, Imran Miah, Yew-Hong Mo, Kerry Morgan, Jessica and Alice Moxley, Aiden Mulcahy, Fiona Mulcahy, Tania Murphy, Moriam Mustapha, Lucy Nightingale, Ify Obi, Adenike Odeleye, Wura Odurinde, Laurence Ody, Folake Ogundeyin, Abayomi Ojo, Fola Oladimeji, Ola Olawe, Lucy Oliver, Michael Oloyede, Yemisi Omolewa, Tope Oni, Alexander and Dominic Paneth, Kim Peterson, Mai-Anh Peterson, Patrice Picard, Alice Purton, Josephina Quayson, Pedro Henrique Queiroz, Brandon Rayment, Alexandra Richards, Leigh Richards, Jamie Rosso, Nida Sayeed, Alex Simons, Charlie Simpson, Aaron Singh, Antonino Sipiano, Justine Spiers, Marlon Stewart, Tom Swaine Jameson, Catherine Tolstoy, Maria Tsang, Nicola and Sarah Twiner, Frankie David Viner, Sophie Louise Viner, Nhat Han Vong, Rupert and Roxy Walton, Devika Webb, George Wheeler, Claudius Wilson, Andreas Wiseman. Kate Yudt, Tanyel Yusef.

Contributors: Petra Boase, Stephanie Donaldson, Sarah Maxwell, Michael Purton, Thomasina Smith, Sally Walton.

Gratitude also to Hampden Gurney School, Walnut Tree Walk Primary School and St John the Baptist C. of E. School.

The authors would like to thank the following for their assistance in providing materials and advice – Boots; Dylon Consumer Advice; Head Gardener, Knightsbridge; Lady Jayne; Mason Pearson, Kent; Molton Brown; Tesco. Special thanks to Justin of Air Circus; 'Smiley Face' from Theatre Crew, Tunbridge Wells; and the Bristol Juggling Convention.